Francis Frith's
HEREFORDSHIRE
Living Memories

photographs of the mid twentieth century

Francis Frith's

HEREFORDSHIRE
Living Memories

Dorothy Nicolle

First published in the United Kingdom in 2002 by The Francis Frith Collection

Hardback Edition 2002 ISBN 1-85937-514-6

Paperback Edition 2005 ISBN 1-84589-107-4

British Library Cataloguing in Publication Data

Herefordshire Living Memories
Dorothy Nicolle

The Francis Frith Collection
Frith's Barn, Teffont,
Salisbury, Wiltshire SP3 5QP
Tel: +44 (0) 1722 716 376
Email: info@francisfrith.co.uk
www.francisfrith.co.uk

Printed and bound in Great Britain

Front Cover: HEREFORD, Widemarsh Street c1950 H74032t

*The colour-tinting is for illustrative purposes only, and is not intended
to be historically accurate*

Aerial photographs reproduced under licence from
Simmons Aerofilms Limited.
Historical Ordnance Survey maps reproduced under licence from
Homecheck.co.uk
Every attempt has been made to contact copyright holders of
illustrative material. We will be happy to give full
acknowledegement in future editions for any items not credited.
Any information should be directed to The Francis Frith Collection.

AS WITH ANY HISTORICAL DATABASE THE FRITH ARCHIVE IS
CONSTANTLY BEING CORRECTED AND IMPROVED AND THE
PUBLISHERS WOULD WELCOME INFORMATION ON OMISSIONS OR INACCURACIES

contents

Francis Frith: Victorian Pioneer	7
Frith's Archive - A Unique Legacy	10
Herefordshire - An Introduction	12
The North-West of the County	16
Eastern Herefordshire	58
The Heart of Herefordshire	76
The South of the County	92
Index	115
Free Mounted Print Voucher	119

Francis Frith: Victorian Pioneer

Francis Frith, Victorian founder of the world-famous photographic archive, was a complex and multi-talented man. A devout Quaker and a highly successful Victorian businessman, he was both philosophic by nature and pioneering in outlook.

By 1855 Francis Frith had already established a wholesale grocery business in Liverpool, and sold it for the astonishing sum of £200,000, which is the equivalent today of over £15,000,000. Now a very rich man, he was able to indulge his passion for travel. As a child he had pored over travel books written by early explorers, and his fancy and imagination had been stirred by family holidays to the sublime mountain regions of Wales and Scotland. 'What lands of spirit-stirring and enriching scenes and places!' he had written. He was to return to these scenes of grandeur in later years to 'recapture the thousands of vivid and tender memories', but with a different purpose. Now in his thirties, and captivated by the new science of photography, Frith set out on a series of pioneering journeys to the Nile regions that occupied him from 1856 until 1860.

Intrigue and Adventure

He took with him on his travels a specially-designed wicker carriage that acted as both dark-room and sleeping chamber. These far-flung journeys were packed with intrigue and adventure. In his life story, written when he was sixty-three, Frith tells of being held captive by bandits, and of fighting 'an awful midnight battle to the very point of surrender with a deadly pack of hungry, wild dogs'. Sporting flowing Arab costume, Frith arrived at Akaba by camel sixty years before Lawrence, where he encountered 'desert princes and rival sheikhs, blazing with jewel-hilted swords'.

During these extraordinary adventures he was assiduously exploring the desert regions bordering the Nile and patiently recording the antiquities and peoples with his camera. He was the first photographer to venture beyond the sixth cataract. Africa was still the mysterious 'Dark Continent', and Stanley and Livingstone's historic meeting was a decade into the future. The conditions for picture taking confound belief. He laboured for hours in his wicker dark-room in the sweltering heat of the desert, while the volatile chemicals fizzed dangerously in their trays. Often he was forced to work in remote tombs and caves where conditions were cooler. Back in London he exhibited his photographs and was 'rapturously cheered' by members of the Royal Society. His reputation as a photographer was made overnight. An eminent modern historian has likened their impact on the population of the time to that on our own generation of the first photographs taken on the surface of the moon.

Venture of a Life-Time

Characteristically, Frith quickly spotted the opportunity to create a new business as a specialist publisher of photographs. He lived in an era of immense and sometimes violent change. For the poor in the early part of Victoria's reign work was a drudge and the hours long, and people had precious little free time to enjoy themselves. Most had no transport other than a cart or gig at their disposal, and had not travelled far beyond the boundaries of their own town or village. However,

by the 1870s, the railways had threaded their way across the country, and Bank Holidays and half-day Saturdays had been made obligatory by Act of Parliament. All of a sudden the ordinary working man and his family were able to enjoy days out and see a little more of the world.

With characteristic business acumen, Francis Frith foresaw that these new tourists would enjoy having souvenirs to commemorate their days out. In 1860 he married Mary Ann Rosling and set out with the intention of photographing every city, town and village in Britain. For the next thirty years he travelled the country by train and by pony and trap, producing fine photographs of seaside resorts and beauty spots that were keenly bought by millions of Victorians. These prints were painstakingly pasted into family albums and pored over during the dark nights of winter, rekindling precious memories of summer excursions.

The Rise of Frith & Co

Frith's studio was soon supplying retail shops all over the country. To meet the demand he gathered about him a small team of photographers, and published the work of independent artist-photographers of the calibre of Roger Fenton and Francis Bedford. In order to gain some understanding of the scale of Frith's business one only has to look at the catalogue issued by Frith & Co in 1886: it runs to some 670 pages, listing not only many thousands of views of the British Isles but also many photographs of most European countries, and China, Japan, the USA and Canada – note the sample page shown on page 9 from the hand-written Frith & Co ledgers detailing pictures taken. By 1890 Frith had created the greatest specialist photographic publishing company in the

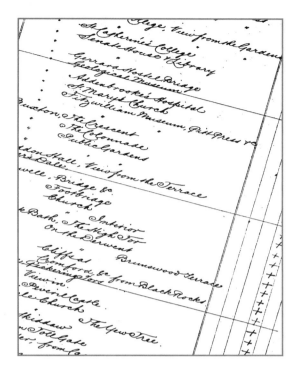

year after Frith's death, a new card measuring 5.5 x 3.5 inches became the standard format, but it was not until 1902 that the divided back came into being, with address and message on one face and a full-size illustration on the other. Frith & Co were in the vanguard of postcard development, and Frith's sons Eustace and Cyril continued their father's monumental task, expanding the number of views offered to the public and recording more and more places in Britain, as the coasts and countryside were opened up to mass travel.

Francis Frith died in 1898 at his villa in Cannes, his great project still growing. The archive he created continued in business for another seventy years. By 1970 it contained over a third of a million pictures of 7,000 cities, towns and villages. The massive photographic record Frith has left to us stands as a living monument to a special and very remarkable man.

world, with over 2,000 outlets – more than the combined number that Boots and WH Smith have today! The picture on the right shows the Frith & Co display board at Ingleton in the Yorkshire Dales (left of window). Beautifully constructed with a mahogany frame and gilt inserts, it could to a dozen local scenes.

Postcard Bonanza

The ever-popular holiday postcard we know today took many years to develop. In 1870 the Post Office issued the first plain cards, with a pre-printed stamp on one face. In 1894 they allowed other publishers' cards to be sent through the mail with an attached adhesive halfpenny stamp. Demand grew rapidly, and in 1895 a new size of postcard was permitted called the court card, but there was little room for illustration. In 1899, a

Frith's Archive: A Unique Legacy

FRANCIS FRITH'S legacy to us today is of immense significance and value, for the magnificent archive of evocative photographs he created provides a unique record of change in 7,000 cities, towns and villages throughout Britain over a century and more. Frith and his fellow studio photographers revisited locations many times down the years to update their views, compiling for us an enthralling and colourful pageant of British life and character.

We tend to think of Frith's sepia views of Britain as nostalgic, for most of us use them to conjure up memories of places in our own lives with which we have family associations. It often makes us forget that to Francis Frith they were records of daily life as it was actually being lived in the cities, towns and villages of his day. The Victorian age was one of great and often bewildering change for ordinary people, and though the pictures evoke an impression of slower times, life was as busy and hectic as it is today.

We are fortunate that Frith was a photographer of the people, dedicated to recording the minutiae of everyday life. For it is this sheer wealth of visual data, the painstaking chronicle of changes in dress, transport, street layouts, buildings, housing, engineering and landscape that captivates us so much today. His remarkable images offer us a powerful link with the past and with the lives of our ancestors.

Today's Technology

Computers have now made it possible for Frith's many thousands of images to be accessed almost instantly. In the Frith archive today, each photograph is carefully 'digitised' then stored on a CD Rom. Frith archivists can locate a single photograph amongst thousands within seconds. Views can be catalogued and sorted under a variety of categories of place and content to the immediate benefit of researchers.

Inexpensive reference prints can be created for them at the touch of a mouse button, and a wide range of books and other printed materials assembled and published for a wider, more general readership - in the next twelve months over a hundred Frith local history titles will be published! The day-to-day workings of the archive are very different from how they were in Francis Frith's time: imagine the herculean task of sorting through eleven tons of glass negatives as Frith had to do to locate a particular sequence of pictures!

See Frith at www.francisfrith.co.uk

Yet the archive still prides itself on maintaining the same high standards of excellence laid down by Francis Frith, including the painstaking cataloguing and indexing of every view.

It is curious to reflect on how the internet now allows researchers in America and elsewhere greater instant access to the archive than Frith himself ever enjoyed. Many thousands of individual views can be called up on screen within seconds on one of the Frith internet sites, enabling people living continents away to revisit the streets of their ancestral home town, or view places in Britain where they have enjoyed holidays. Many overseas researchers welcome the chance to view special theme selections, such as transport, sports, costume and ancient monuments.

We are certain that Francis Frith would have heartily approved of these modern developments in imaging techniques, for he himself was always working at the very limits of Victorian photographic technology.

The Value of the Archive Today

Because of the benefits brought by the computer, Frith's images are increasingly studied by social historians, by researchers into genealogy and ancestry, by architects, town planners, and by teachers and schoolchildren involved in local history projects.

In addition, the archive offers every one of us an opportunity to examine the places where we and our families have lived and worked down the years. Highly successful in Frith's own era, the archive is now, a century and more on, entering a new phase of popularity.

The Past in Tune with the Future

Historians consider the Francis Frith Collection to be of prime national importance. It is the only archive of its kind remaining in private ownership and has been valued at a million pounds. However, this figure is now rapidly increasing as digital technology enables more and more people around the world to enjoy its benefits.

Francis Frith's archive is now housed in an historic timber barn in the beautiful village of Teffont in Wiltshire. Its founder would not recognize the archive office as it is today. In place of the many thousands of dusty boxes containing glass plate negatives and an all-pervading odour of photographic chemicals, there are now ranks of computer screens. He would be amazed to watch his images travelling round the world at unimaginable speeds through network and internet lines.

The archive's future is both bright and exciting. Francis Frith, with his unshakeable belief in making photographs available to the greatest number of people, would undoubtedly approve of what is being done today with his lifetime's work. His photographs, depicting our shared past, are now bringing pleasure and enlightenment to millions around the world a century and more after his death.

Herefordshire - An Introduction

DANIEL DEFOE ONCE said of Herefordshire, 'the people of the county are a diligent and laborious people, chiefly addicted to husbandry. They boast, perhaps not without reason, that they have the finest wool, the best hops and the richest cyder in all Britain. One would hardly expect so pleasant and fruitful a county as this, so near the barren mountains of Wales'.

Although written some 200 years ago, this is probably the way the county is still seen by just about all its visitors, even today. Herefordshire is a county of rich pastureland and blossom-covered orchards, with footpaths that meander through leafy valleys and over open hillsides with the most glorious views. Spaced around the edge of the county are small country market towns that still have individual shops, as opposed to large superstores, while dotted throughout are attractive, friendly villages. In other words, it's the kind of countryside that we all imagine when we go overseas and think of home. Herefordshire epitomises an almost 'in-born' memory that many people have of England at its best.

It is a view of England that is very evident in these photographs from the Francis Frith Collection. They were all taken within the last 50 years – a period that has seen more changes in England than any period before. And yet, happily,

the character of traditional old England remains today to be discovered by the modern visitor to the county.

And that's not all Herefordshire has to offer. There are castles galore, from the genuine old ruins at Goodrich, Longtown and Wigmore, to the modern 'fakes' such as Eastnor Castle. Herefordshire also has some stunningly beautiful houses, many of which are virtually unknown outside of the county. Houses such as Hellens near Much Marcle or Berrington Hall and Croft Castle in the north. Perhaps Herefordshire's real gems, however, are its churches. There is, of course, the beautiful cathedral in Hereford itself, and the ancient chained library housing medieval treasures including the Mappa Mundi with its strange view of the world. But, for me, the real riches of Herefordshire are its small churches, especially Kilpeck, covered in early carvings, and the 'wedding cake' church at Shobden.

Herefordshire is a county where time has definitely left its mark in many different ways.

But what about the people who live here? Herefordshire is much more than merely a rural tourist attraction. There is no denying, however, that its rural background is still the basis for the way of life of many of its modern inhabitants. For example, Herefordshire has always been associated with cider and, to this day, cider is still a major product of the county. Bulmers is the largest manufacturer of cider in the world, producing around 56 million gallons a year. Nor is it the only company based here. Others include Westons (like Bulmers founded in the 1880s) and Dunkerton's, specialising in 'organic' ciders.

For many years, cider has given Herefordshire a reputation for the longevity of its people. When visiting the county in the early 1600s, James I was once entertained by a group of 10 Morris dancers. It was said that their combined age was more than 1,000 years. And in Abbey Dore church, there is a memorial to an Elizabeth Lewis who is reputed to have been 141 when she died.

One particularly famous Herefordshire son, who lived to the ripe old age of 97, was John Abel. Born in the reign of Elizabeth I, he became known as the King's Carpenter - the King being Charles I - during the Civil War. In the mid-1600s, he was credited as having 'covered the border with beautiful timbered buildings'. A number of these still survive around the county, along with those built by the many unknown carpenters who preceded him, in some cases by several centuries.

The county of Herefordshire is almost circular in shape with the city of Hereford in the centre. Hereford may be a relatively small city but it has held city status for considerably longer than most other of our English cities. Named as the settlement by 'the ford where the army crosses', Hereford's history as a settlement can be traced

back to at least Saxon times. It became an early centre for the new Christian religion adopted by the Anglo-Saxons and, in the 7th century, the first church was built on the site now occupied by the great cathedral.

Over the years, an important trading centre grew up beside the cathedral, around the market area now known as High Town. Its long history has resulted in the enchanting place that Hereford is today. Small enough to be easily explored by the visitor, it is large enough to offer everything required by its present day permanent community. It also is an important centre for the arts and has been a home to the Three Choirs Festival since the early 1700s.

Hereford dominates its county from the heart, with roads leading in all directions towards the towns that encircle it – almost all of which are equidistant from the city and from each other. Rather like the spokes of a wheel, each of these towns sits right beside or very close to the county boundary.

Starting from the north-west, we have Kington. Today the border with Wales is just a couple of miles beyond the town. At one time, though, the border demarcated by Offa's Dyke cut right through what is now the town centre. Although comparatively quiet now, Kington must have been a vitally important town in Saxon times, protecting the border from those marauding Welsh! In recent

years, before licensing laws were changed, it benefited every Sunday from the fact that all the pubs just across the border in Wales were closed, while those in Kington, within England, were open. The marauding Welsh were still coming across the border but for a different reason!

Directly north of Hereford, is the town of Leominster, Herefordshire's second largest. Like Hereford, this town probably started out as a religious centre at much the same time as the city. The minster church established here was later to become an important priory, but it was the market beside it that brought real wealth to Leominster - in the form of wool. Evidence of this wealth can still be seen in the lavish carving detail on the church, the main part of which was fortunate to survive the Dissolution in the 16th century.

Travelling eastwards, we come to Bromyard – another market town, this time traditionally linked with the cultivation of hops. In past years, when it was time for the crop to be harvested, the area would be flooded with workers from all over the Midlands and Wales, combining a holiday (of sorts) with a chance to earn some money.

Continuing clockwise around the county, we turn southwards to arrive at Ledbury. This is a particularly pretty little town and regularly earns an income from film companies searching for picturesque and historic settings for their films. This in turn attracts visitors to the area, many of

whom have an interest in poetry – each July the town hosts a poetry festival.

The beautiful town of Ross-on-Wye, perched on its sandstone cliff, completes the circle of towns around Hereford. Situated in the south-east of the county, its name derives from the Welsh 'rhos' – meaning a hill or a promontory. Some prefer the explanation, however, that the name describes how the town appears to rise up from the river. Others argue that it's a reference to the rose-coloured sandstone on which the town rests. Whatever meaning you prefer, the town's setting overlooking the River Wye is quite perfect.

With Ross, however, the idea that all Herefordshire's towns encircle the cathedral city seems to come to an end. There are no further towns between here and Kington - at least not in Herefordshire itself. Instead, the towns of Monmouth, Abergavenny and Hay-on-Wye continue the circular pattern, only they are all in Wales instead. Here, in wilder hill country, all these towns sit beside the main routes into Wales.

Nestling amongst the hills, numerous villages and hamlets can be found. In fact throughout the county, there are dozens of attractive villages with evocative names like Much Marcle, Moreton-on-Lugg and Wormlow Tump. Despite their beauty, these villages still have problems such as the closing of local schools and villages shops, post offices and pubs. The ever increasing role of the automobile, so clearly evident in these photographs, has led to car dependence in all too many aspects of our lives.

Although taken relatively recently, enormous changes have taken place since these pictures were taken. Here in Herefordshire, many changes can be seen, and these have not always been for the best. Recent years have witnessed misfortune for the whole agricultural economy, with rural counties such as Herefordshire being particularly hard hit. It is difficult for many people to look forward with optimism, although the changes reflected in old photographs such as these do serve to remind us that the world has a habit of turning full circle. I like to think that Herefordshire's people can indeed look forward into the future with optimism.

The North-West of The County

Leintwardine, The Bathing Pool c1955 L214022
For many of us, photographs taken in the 1950s
and 1960s reminds us of our childhood days.
For me, this photograph is a particularly special
reminder of carefree summer days – it almost
never rained, did it?

◀ **Leintwardine
The Bank c1955** L214016
Such a peaceful setting
could never be associated
with warfare ... but
Leintwardine was once the
home of Sir Banastre
Tarleton who fought in the
American War of
Independence and whose
reputation has recently
been torn to shreds (unfairly
in my opinion) in the film,
The Patriot, starring Mel
Gibson.

◄ Leintwardine
The Village c1955
L214029
Leintwardine straddles an ancient Roman settlement, Bravinium, along Watling Street, (not to be confused with the better known Watling Street that leads from London to Wroxeter). The church in the centre of the village sits on Roman earthworks and Roman tiles and bricks have been discovered beneath the chancel.

▼ Leintwardine, Thatched
Cottage c1955 L214032
This thatched cottage sits at the northern end of the village and was once a pub whose custom came from those travelling to and from Shropshire. Today the house is instantly recognisable but very much prettier than in this photograph.

◄ Kingsland
The Village c1955
K97013
A scene that was once familiar in many villages up and down the country. Notice the petrol pump on the right. Roadside pumps such as this have nearly all disappeared, although there are a couple still in use elsewhere in the county.

◀ **Eardisland**
Staick House c1960
E105040
A former rectory, the great hall of this beautiful building dates from around 1300, although parts were added later in the 16th and 17th centuries. It's now in an extremely ruinous state and there are fears that it may be beyond saving.

Kingsland
The Angel Inn c1955
K97008

There are a number of lovely timber-framed buildings in this village, and many more that were once of timber, until a brick façade was added at a later date. The pub is one such example of this, although its timbers have since been partially exposed once again.

▼ Eardisland, The Ford c1960 E105042

The River Arrow meanders over a wide flood plain and most villages in the area sit well above its banks. However Eardisland, for some reason, is situated right beside the river. Its name is thought to derive partly from a Welsh word 'llion' meaning floods, and perhaps the floods and the marshy land around about was originally an advantage, enabling the villagers to hide from attackers.

◄ Eardisland, The Bridge c1955 E105024

One of several villages on Herefordshire's 'black and white trail', Eardisland has also been voted one of the prettiest in the country. Strangely, in an area where most old timber houses are having their plaster removed, the black and white house pictured here has since been plastered and painted white.

Eardisland, River Arrow c1955 E105028
The Bridge Stores have since been converted into a private house. There is a dispute in the village over ownership of the river bank in the foreground and, consequently, it looks somewhat unkempt these days.

Eardisland, The Village c1960 E105037
The garden in the foreground is that of a house aptly named Arrow Bank, a beautifully situated house now used for a bed and breakfast business. Notice the white gate held open beside the lane – in the deeds for Arrow Bank it is stated that this gate must be closed once a year.

Eardisland, The Village c1955 E105019

Just beyond the cross, in the heart of the village, there is now an old restored AA telephone box. The building on the right has recently been restored too – it was originally a dovecote and is now a small museum. Across the road, the black and white building was once a school, and there is an old whipping post in the garden beside the bridge.

Pembridge c1960 P172021

There can't be many village shops that can claim to have been trading for more than 200 years. The timber building on the left can make just that claim. Known as The Olde Steppes, this shop was in business in 1777. Prior to that time it is thought to have been a rectory, Pembridge's church sits on the hillside just behind it.

**Pembridge
The Village c1965**
P172023
The cottages on the right are almshouses and were built in the 1600s. Notice the flights of steps leading up to each door. The building in the centre, to the right of the Esso garage, was once a pub called the Greyhound – it now houses tea rooms and a visitor centre.

▼ **Pembridge, The Church c1960** P172024
St Mary's church is best known for its most unusual detached three-storey belfry. It dates from the 13th century and has an octagonal ground floor with the upper floors supported on four posts, each of which is a single tree-trunk.

▼ **Pembridge, The New Inn c1955** P172019
The delightful little market shelter in the foreground dates from the 16th century. Legend has it that there was once an upper floor that was used as a lock-up for local miscreants, but this is generally thought to be unlikely.

▲ **Pembridge c1965**
P172020
The New Inn can be seen in this photograph, on the right-hand side of the road. 'New' isn't a very accurate description of the inn – but it was new once, when it was built in the early 1600s. There was an even earlier inn on this site, where a treaty was signed in 1461 after the Battle of Mortimer's Cross.

◀ **Pembridge, Red Lion Corner c1965** P172015
The Red Lion is the building on the right. Like so many other local timber buildings, it now has a brick façade. The survival of so many timber buildings is a reminder that by the 17th and 18th centuries, the village's fortunes had declined. Elsewhere people paid to follow fashion and cover their houses with bricks; here that was a luxury few could afford.

Above:

Pembridge c1955 P172016

This view looks into the village as you would see it if you were approaching from Kington. The building on the left is the appropriately named Westend Cottage which was built in the 17th century.

Right:

Lyonshall, St Michael's Church c1965 L218008

Lyonshall's church sits some little distance from the heart of the present village. Apparently the original village was situated here, but after the Black Death in the mid 14th century those villagers that survived moved almost half a mile away.

Lyonshall, The Village c1965 L218004
This is where they moved to. Today Lyonshall still boasts one pub, The Royal George, just beyond the car in this photograph. There is a sign on the lamppost advertising 'Lyons tea' which seems very apt in Lyonshall.

Kington, The Golf Club c1965 K98088
The Kington Golf Club was established in 1924 and there can be few golf clubs that occupy such a magnificent site. It is located on the slopes of Bradnor Hill, just to the north of Kington, with wonderful views in all directions even if the golfers in the picture seem to be ignoring them.

▼ **Kington, View from Bradnor Hill c1965** K98054
Amongst the many hills that can be seen from the summit
of Bradnor Hill, Hergest Ridge lies towards the south west.
This is a name that will be familiar to fans of Mike Oldfield's music
and it is easy to see how this countryside could inspire anyone.

▼ **Kington, High Street c1960** K98080
The town is known as Kington simply because it was the King's town
at one time and it is generally assumed that the king in question was
Edward the Confessor. However, Offa's Dyke passes right beside the
town and so some people have suggested that the king is actually King
Offa who reigned some 250 years earlier.

▲ **Kington, Town Centre
c1955** K98043
It was once said of
Kington that 'if you
passed through at any
time other than on
Market Day you would
have seen the shops
open, and the houses
open, and a few persons
walking about the streets
with their eyes open; but
all the shops and the
houses and the people
therein were asleep …
(and) the quacking of a
duck could be heard
from one end to the
other'.

◀ **Kington, Church Street c1955** K98029
Kington was also once described as having a 'maze of narrow streets ... where too many of the old houses have been refronted, but still have the attraction of a wildly irregular skyline'. There have been relatively few changes here, one of the best being that the Imperial Café is now a second hand bookshop called Castle Hill Books.

Kington, Church Street c1955 K98061
The evil spirit of Black Vaughan once terrorised the local people here. One day 13 parsons attempted to exorcise the ghost, but when his spirit appeared they were so scared that 12 of them fainted. Fortunately the last parson standing managed to reduce the evil spirit to the size of a bluebottle, imprisoned it in his snuff-box and then buried it.

Kington, Lady Hawkins School c1960 K98084
Lady Margaret Hawkins, after whom the school is named, was the wife of Sir John Hawkins, one of the commanders fighting against the Spanish Armada in 1588. She bequeathed £800 'to keep a free school in Kington … for the instructing and teaching of youths and children in literature and good education'.

Eardisley, Upper House Farm c1950 E106009
Like Pembridge, the village of Eardisley is mainly built along one long street and, like Pembridge also, there are some lovely buildings along that street. It is fitting that it is known as one of the villages on Herefordshire's 'black and white trail'.

Eardisley, Whitney Road c1955 E106023
The village's only junction is shown here. Although Arthur Conan Doyle set his novel 'The Hound of the Baskervilles' in Dartmoor, he got his inspiration here – the Baskerville family once owned Eardisley's castle and the story of the black hound is a local legend in nearby Kington. Presumably Doyle thought that the countryside here was far too peaceful a setting for his story!

Eardisley c1950 E106010
The small ivy-covered structure beside the road still survives
although the ivy has since been removed. It looks like a small bus
shelter, but it actually houses the village water pump which,
incidentally, can still be seen inside it.

Eardisley c1955 E106028
Brierley, the family butcher, is no longer here and the shop premises have been absorbed into the house behind, known as the Olde House.

Whitney, the Church and Wye Valley c1955 W307307
Today this view hasn't changed at all. Despite increases in population and the subsequent rise in road traffic, Herefordshire still manages to retain an aura of peacefulness and serenity, exemplified in this photograph.

Whitney, The Church c1950 W307304
The present church sits some way above the River Wye. There was an earlier church nearer to the water but it was washed away when the river flooded, so this church dates from 1740. However much was salvaged from the old church and its old Norman font still survives.

Whitney, The Church Interior c1950 W307308
The interior of St Peter and St Paul's church is much the same, although sadly, in my opinion, the 'God Is Love' script has been painted out. Notice, also, the beautifully carved pulpit.

Whitney, Court and Rectory c1950 W307302
The Court, built in 1902, is the building just visible on the hillside in the distance. The rectory, now known as Wardour House, is in the foreground.

Whitney, The Boat Inn c1955 W307004
The Boat Inn, as its name suggests, sits right on the bank of the River Wye. Perhaps its name implies that there was once a ferry crossing here long ago. In 1802, however, a wooden toll bridge was built nearby which is still in regular use today.

Winforton, The Church c1955 W310019
St Michael's church stands on a site that has been used for various churches for well over 1,000 years. The present church was restored by the Victorians but still has its medieval stone tower and 16th-century timber belfry.

Winforton, Old Cross Restaurant (1200AD) c1955 W310022
Winforton has been described as a typical 'farm village' and this building would once have been the home of a very well-to-do farmer. Although housing a restaurant at the time this picture was taken, the building has since been converted and split into two private houses.

Winforton, Old Cross Restaurant, the Original Fireplace c1955 W310014 (top)
& the Dining Room c1955 W310013 (below)
The interior will have changed considerably since the restaurant was here. However it is interesting to compare it with a similar establishment today. Sadly, few restaurants have such smart, crisp, white tablecloths and napkins these days, even if those chairs were rather uncomfortable!

Top: **Winforton Court c1955** W310021
This magnificent building stands right beside the road but is hidden by what is now a much taller, and thicker, hedge. It was in this village, in an old malt house, that pictures from the National Gallery were once stored, well away from London's air raids, during the Second World War.

Below: **Sarnesfield, The Church c1950** S769036
The church in Sarnesfield has a dovecote in its tower, large enough for roughly 1,000 doves. Here also is the tomb of John Abel; he was a master carpenter in the 17th century and his buildings are dotted throughout the county. He died in 1674 at the age of 97 and carved his own tombstone, depicting himself kneeling with his two wives beside him.

Weobley, The Ley c1965 W304096
Built in 1589 (the year after the Spanish Armada) the Ley is one of Herefordshire's largest and most beautiful timber houses. Timber buildings were always notoriously draughty but the fireplaces encased in those enormous chimneys must have provided plenty of heat!

Weobley, The Village c1950 W304059
When Leland visited Weobley in 1540 he described it as 'a market-town where there is a goodly castle, but somewhat in decay'. The castle has now gone but the village is quite, quite beautiful and ranks as one of the best black and white villages anywhere in the country.

▼ **Weobley, Ye Olde Salutation Inn c1955** W304047

In 1999 Weobley was named the 'National Village of the Year' and, in order to celebrate both this and the Millennium that followed, a sculpture was erected in the garden area in the foreground of this picture. For a black and white village, the sculpture appropriately depicts a bird, Magnus the Magpie.

▼ **Weobley, The Post Office c1960** W304115

Judging by the sign above the door, many tourists were already coming to Weobley in the 1960s. The sign reads '16th century Tudor Tea Room. Afternoon Teas. Home Made Cakes. Pottery. Gifts'. It is still the village post office.

▲ **Weobley, The Unicorn Inn c1960** W304119

The Unicorn is one of several beautiful, old timber inns in Weobley. When visiting Weobley, Charles I stayed in the Unicorn Inn, but that Unicorn was a totally different building which later became a house called 'The Throne'.

◄ **Weobley**
Old Grammar School c1960

W304083

A guidebook in 1795 described Weobley as having 'a few small streets meanly constructed, without either market or traffic'. Certainly by the early 19th century this was a village in decline. As it turned out this was rather fortunate, because lack of money to rebuild or alter its buildings is one of the reasons Weobley is such an attractive place today.

Weobley
Kington Road c1950 W304006
This house has recently been restored revealing even more timber
frames than can be seen in this photograph. Instead of being black
and white, it has been painted black and pink which offends some
purists. In fact, traditionally, houses were sometimes painted that
colour, the pink deriving from cow's blood that was used as a dye.

Weobley, The Oldest Cottage in England c1955 W304058
The claim that this is the oldest cottage in England would probably receive short shrift today but it is certainly an interesting building. Notice the enormous timbers in the gable end – these would have been cut by slicing down the entire length of a single tree. The building now forms part of the Red Lion Inn which can be seen just beyond it.

Weobley, The Orchard c1955 W304041
In 1586 Camden said that Weobley had 'more fair cellars than most market towns of its bigness in England'. Here we see a nearby orchard in springtime with the ewes and their lambs grazing below the trees. In May, when the apple blossom is in flower, the black and white trail could more accurately be termed the black, white and pink trail.

Dilwyn
The Church and
Village c1960 D123001
The name Dilwyn is
delightful – apparently
it means a secret, shady
or lovely place and
each of these adjectives
could well be used to
describe this little
village.

Hope under Dinmore, The Church c1955 H264008
With the growth in importance of the busy A49, the village of Hope has been virtually cut off from its church. Today it would be a brave man who would walk across the main road just visible here. Consequently there is now an underpass just in front of the church.

Hope under Dinmore, Arkwright's Almshouses c1960 H264011
Nearby Hampton Court became the home of the Arkwright family, the well-known cotton spinning industrialists. The family were great benefactors to the village, hence the name of these almshouses. Notice the man working in his vegetable plot on the right of the picture.

Hope under Dinmore, The Church c1955 H264006
One particularly sad monument in St Mary's church is dedicated to a small child who died after choking on a cherry stone in 1708. The memorial even shows the child with the cherry in his mouth.

▼ **Hope under Dinmore, The Village c1955** H264010
The word 'hope' was an old Welsh word meaning a valley and so
here we have the settlement in the valley under the hill fort, 'mawr'
being a reference to the ancient hill fort at one end of the hill. Today
this hill is a wonderful place to walk as it is largely taken over by the
Queen's Wood Country Park with an extensive collection of trees
from all over the world.

▼ **Hope under Dinmore, The Fork Road c1955** H264005
At this point the main Leominster to Hereford road starts to climb the
steep hill. Stagecoaches would have been forced to stop here to pay
their toll at the toll house overlooking the junction. Notice the AA
phone box, a common sight around the countryside in the 1950s.

▲ **Hope under Dinmore
Markhams Filling
Station c1955** H264004a
All three petrol pumps in
the photograph are
selling petrol for
different companies.
There is still a petrol
station here today but it
is linked to just one
company. A cup of tea
(see the sign beyond the
pumps) can still be
purchased here too –
there is now a Little Chef
on the site as well.

◄ Hope under Dinmore, Hampton Court c1955
H264001
This beautiful house dates from the early 15th century. Since 1996 the gardens have been beautifully restored and are now open to the public, as is a conservatory now used as a tea-room, which was built by Joseph Paxton, the designer of the Crystal Palace.

Leominster, South Street c1960 L36044
The town's name is pronounced 'Lemster' and this is how the word was sometimes spelt on old milestones. Herefordshire's second largest town, it is most unusual in this part of Britain in that it has never had a castle, either to subdue its inhabitants, or to protect it from its neighbours.

Leominster
Corn Square c1965 L36056
'Lemster ore' was the local name for the wool that came from here. It was so fine in quality that Queen Elizabeth I used it for her stockings. Daniel Defoe described it as 'the finest without exception of any in England' and certainly it was valued at about four times the cost of any wool elsewhere in the country.

▼ **Leominster, Corn Square c1955** L36029

Notice the old Town Hall on the right hand side of the photograph – now sadly destroyed and replaced by an extremely bland 1960s building. The old timber market hall once stood here, built by John Abel in 1633, with magnificent carving detail. Fortunately Abel's building was bought by John Arkwright, the owner of Hampton Court, and has since been re-erected near the church.

▼ **Leominster, High Street c1960** L36043

It looks quiet here now, but once the market at Leominster was so successful that the cities of Hereford and Worcester were jealous of its success. They persuaded Henry III to force Leominster to change its market day from Saturday to Friday. Even so it was still, in the 16th century, described as 'the greatest market town in the county of Hereford'.

▲ **Leominster, West Street c1955** L36014

The large building on the left is The Talbot Hotel, a common name for pubs and hotels in the Welsh Marches. John Talbot, 1st Earl of Shrewsbury, fought in the 100 Years War against the French. Shakespeare described him as 'The Scourge of France' in his play, Henry VI.

◄ **Leominster**
Broad Street c1950 L36002
Daniel Defoe, speaking of Leominster, described it as having 'nothing very remarkable about it, but that it is a well-built, well-inhabited town. This town, besides its fine wool, is noted for the best wheat and consequently the finest bread.' Notice the horse-drawn wagon in the centre of the photograph.

Eastern Herefordshire

Bredenbury Court c1960 B422018
Bredenbury Court was built in the late 1800s and was a private house for a relatively short time before becoming a school in the 1920s. Notice the children reading under the shade of the tree to the left of the picture.

◀ **Bredenbury Court, Arts and Crafts Exhibition c1960** B422022
This is still the school's art room and is instantly recognisable. Notice the wooden flooring – when the house was still privately-owned this room was built as a bowling alley and the floor was specially laid as the bowling lane.

◄ Bredenbury Court Swimming Pool c1960
B422026
All the children in the photographs are girls – when these pictures were taken the school was a primary school for girls who then generally went on to Cheltenham Ladies College. In 1968 it changed to become a school for both boys and girls, St Richard's School, with children from the ages of three to 13 years old.

▼ Bredenbury, View from the School c1955 B422004
This superb view is also virtually unchanged. It looks northwards over the Teme valley and into the neighbouring county of Shropshire.

◄ Bromyard Church of St Peter c1960 B229109
Although much of St Peter's church dates from as recently as the 14th century, there are signs of a much earlier church on the site. Above the doorway is a really beautiful, very early carving of St Peter, complete with his set of keys.

▼ **Bromyard, The Falcon c1965** B229123
The Falcon was once an important coaching inn linking the town with Hereford, Leominster and Worcester. The imposing entrance on the right led to the Midland Bank, though why they should have removed its carved top and replaced it with a very ordinary clock is beyond me!

▼ **Bromyard, The Square c1960** B229080
This is an unusual view of the Square with Church Street beyond. Today the Square has been paved over and has trees planted in it – but it's still used for parking.

▲ **Bromyard, Church Street c1960** B229099
The police station, seen here on the left, now serves as the Bromyard Youth Centre, with the library beside it. The timber building at the far end is known as the Bible House.

◀ **Bromyard, Tower House c1965** B229122
This beautiful building stands in Tower Hill, part of Bromyard that has been virtually cut off from the rest of the town by a new bypass. I suppose we should be thankful that it wasn't pulled down when the bypass was built – several buildings were.

Bromyard, Kidderminster Road c1960 B229101
The country roads in the 1960s look so peaceful – obviously these were not used by heavy traffic and there is no sign of the plethora of white lines that have since been painted. The hills in the distance are the Malvern Hills that form the border of the county with Worcestershire.

Bromyard, Lower Brockhampton c1955 B229089
Lower Brockhampton Farm is so secluded that it sits quietly in its own valley, a mile or so from the nearest road. Today the estate is owned by the National Trust and is a magical place to visit. The little building on the left is a gatehouse sitting astride the moat.

Whitbourne, The Church c1960 W306012
Its name, the white bourne, means the white stream. St John the Baptist's church sits in a wonderfully peaceful setting here. When I visited recently all I could hear was the sound of birds, including a woodpecker peck, peck, pecking.

Whitbourne, 16th century Tudor Tea Rooms c1960 W304136
Whitbourne is only a small settlement and hardly could be said to be on the tourist trail. And yet, we have this picture of its tea rooms. I have been unable to ascertain just where they were. Can any reader help us?

Colwall, Ledbury Road c1945 C216002
This little wooden footbridge seems to lead from nowhere to nowhere but it still survives, though very much the worse for wear nowadays.

Colwall, Jubilee Drive and Worcestershire Beacon c1950 C216003
Colwall's name originally meant 'the place with the cool well' and, of course, to this day the name of the Malvern Hills is synonymous with its spring water. One such well, overlooking the village of Colwell, is right beside the main road and there are often cars parked beside it with people filling plastic bottles with the water. It is particularly good for brewing tea!

Colwall c1960 C216025
Much of Colwall developed in late Victorian times as a result of the building of the railway line and its station. This not only brought convenience for local people - it also enabled visitors to come to the area. The railway helped the Malvern Hills develop as a tourist destination (greatly benefiting Great Malvern, on the other side of the hills).

▼ Colwall, Colwall Park Hotel c1960 C216016

Colwall Park Hotel is situated just by the railway station. It was here in 1926 that the then owner of the hotel, Mrs Scott-Bowden, organised a cricket festival for women – and so founded the National Women's Cricket Association.

▼ Eastnor, The Castle c1950 E107010

Despite its Medieval appearance Eastnor Castle was built between 1810 and 1824. The whole castle cost £85,923 13s 11d, or nearly £9 million in today's money.

▲ Eastnor Castle The Great Hall c1965

E107033

This photograph shows the Great Hall as it was originally intended - displaying a collection of armour and weapons, just as a castle should. It was redesigned in 1986 and now looks much more welcoming, with comfortable sofas in the middle of the room.

◀ Eastnor, Post Office c1965
E107037
This must rank as one of the most picturesque post offices to be found anywhere in the country. Entry is through the door on the left, and the bulk of the building is a private house. It is still, I am glad to say, a post office to this day.

Ledbury, The Park c1955 L132034
The Park, now known as Ledbury Park, provides very up-market accommodation in the heart of the town. It was built in 1595 and was used by Prince Rupert, Charles I's nephew, as his headquarters during the Civil War in 1645. Notice the traffic policeman with his white sleeves – today there is a set of traffic lights at this junction.

▼ Ledbury, New Street c1955 L132049

Just behind the road sign is an entrance to the Feathers Hotel, once an important coaching inn linking the town with Hereford, Worcester, Gloucester and on to London. The coaches travelled at an average speed of about 10mph and were so regular in their time-keeping that people living in the nearby villages could set their watches by them.

▼ Ledbury, High Street c1965 L132064

Here we see the front of the Feathers Hotel on the right. The building was erected in 1565, although the top storey was added later. Bradleys, on the right of the street, is an interesting premises. It now houses a branch of Boots, the chemists, and all the plaster on the front façade has been recently removed revealing a beautiful jettied timber building.

▲ Ledbury, High Street c1955 L132042

Notice how the street widens out as it nears the old market hall. There used to be additional buildings - used as butchers' shops - in the central area, but these were demolished in the early 19th century. The large, open, market area has now been taken over by vehicles, as opposed to animals, coming to market.

◀ **Ledbury, Market House
c1955** L132031
John Abel built a number of
market houses around the
county of Herefordshire,
only a few of which survive.
This is said to be one of his
although there is no
documentation to prove it.
Completed in 1645, it was
used mainly as a corn
market. Originally it had
three storeys but the floor
between the top two has
been removed.

Ledbury, Church Lane c1955 L132033
This view is a regular backdrop for films with an historic setting. The Prince of Wales pub is a delightful timber-framed building, and just beside it, another building has been converted into a Heritage Centre. The church at the end, St Michael's, has holes in its walls said to have been caused by gunfire when there was a skirmish in the church yard during the Civil War.

Ledbury, High Street from Market House c1955 L132043
'I must go down to the sea again, To the lonely sea and the sky.' Ledbury was the birthplace, in 1875, of the future Poet Laureate, John Masefield who is now more closely associated with poems of the sea, which seems strange in a county that is completely land-locked.

Ledbury, Homend c1960 L132058
The tall tower with the clock stands opposite the Market House on a site once occupied by a tannery. It is the Barrett Browning Insitute, built in 1896 to commemorate Elizabeth Barrett Browning, who lived in this area as a child. This connection with both her and John Masefield is remembered at the annual poetry festival.

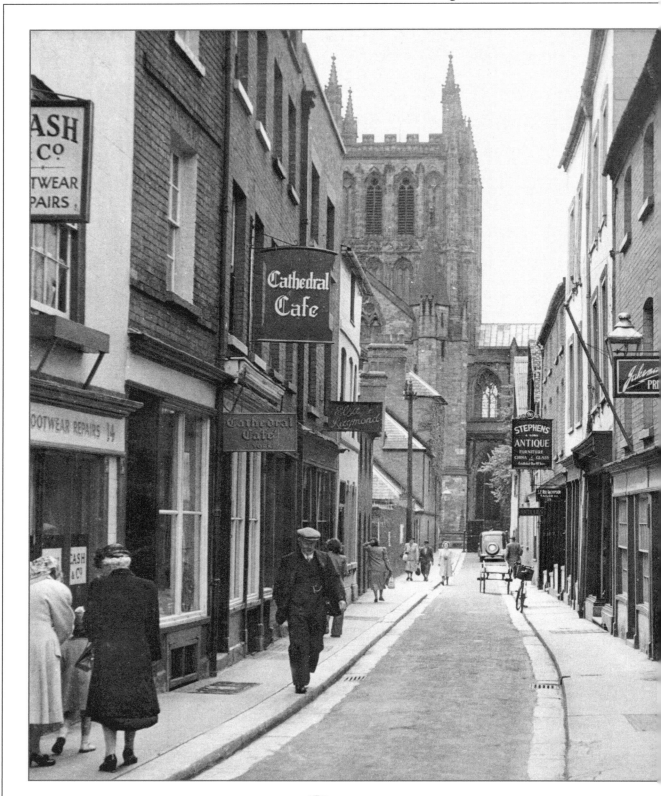

The Heart of Herefordshire

Hereford, Church Street c1950 H74042
This was one of the main streets linking the cathedral with the market area of the town. Interestingly, the pattern of the city's streets still follows the lines laid down even before the time of the Norman Conquest. The cathedral itself, with its tower visible at the end of the street, was founded in the 7th century.

**Hereford, High Town
c1950** H74043
It is interesting to note
that the old market
place was being
overtaken by cars as
early as 1950, and
parking was obviously
already a problem. At
one time, a regulation
stated that all visitors to
Hereford had to leave
their horses at their
lodgings before going to
the market place.
Today this area is totally
pedestrianised.

▼ **Hereford, The Old House and High Town c1950** H74045
The Old House dates from 1612 and was originally a guildhall for the city's butchers. More recently it housed a branch of Lloyds Bank, who gave the building to the city in 1927. Today it is a most delightful museum. The new Lloyds Bank is the imposing building with the columns on the left of the photograph.

▼ **Hereford, St Peter's Square c1950** H74030
Standing beyond the market area of High Town, near to the Shire Hall, St Peter's is the civic church of Hereford. It was founded in 1070 by Walter de Lacy, who later died as a result of falling from the battlements while on a tour of inspection.

▲ **Hereford, Commercial Road c1950** H74036
The old city of Hereford was contained by the River Wye to the south and the town walls to the north. Today a ring road loosely follows the line where the old city walls once stood, criss crossed with radial roads. Commercial Road is one such road - the junction pictured here is always busy and controlled now by traffic lights.

◀ **Hereford**
The Kerry Arms Hotel and Commercial Road c1950
H74037
This view is of the same road junction, but from the opposite direction. 'The Kerry', as its now called, sits between Commercial Road on the right and Union Street. It is interesting to note that this section of Commercial Road (now pedestrianised) was already a one-way route.

Hereford Widemarsh Street c1950 H74032
Widemarsh Street is another of the city's radial roads leading to the north from High Town. This scene has hardly changed at all although the street is now a one-way route; here we can see vehicles moving in all directions, which must have been chaotic even then.

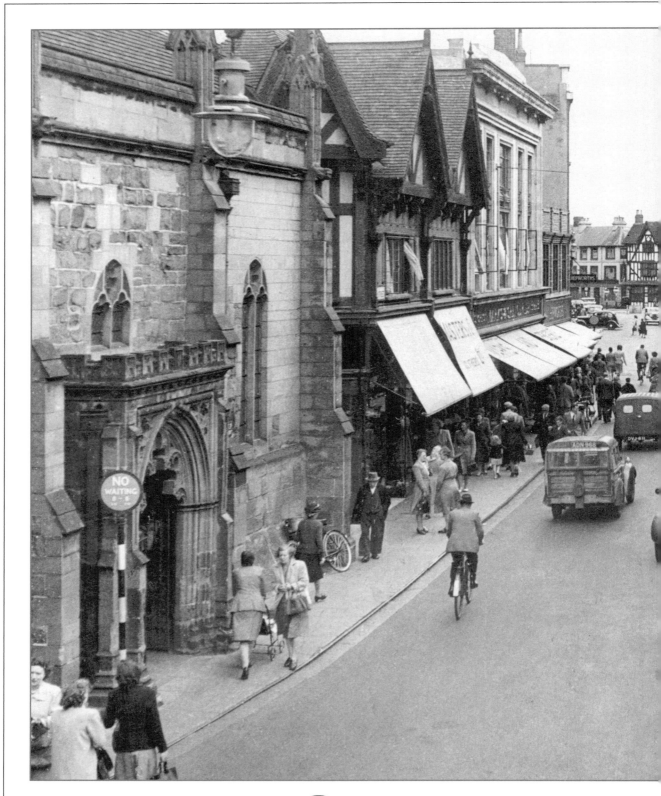

Hereford, High Street c1950 H74039
All Saints'church on the left is a wonderful example of how churches can continue to be houses of worship, while changing their role slightly to suit modern demands. The interior of the church has been recently restored, complete with a coffee shop, and is a wonderful example of just how well modern interpretations of ancient buildings can work.

Hereford, High Town c1950 H74034
The spire of All Saints' church in this photograph doesn't look quite true and, in fact, it does indeed have a slight kink in it. Notice the building on the right with the clock tower – this is the Market Hall built in 1861 and described by Pevsner as 'a kind of free English Wren-Gibbs style, handled without much respect'.

◄ **Madley, The Old Cross and Town House c1955** M364003
The cross here is said to mark the place where St Dubricius was born at some time in the 5th century. According to the historian, Geoffrey of Monmouth, Dubricius (sometimes also known as Dyfrig) was present at King Arthur's coronation and was the founder of a monastery near Ross-on-Wye and several churches in the county.

◀ **Hereford, Eign Gate c1950** H74038
Daniel Defoe described Hereford in 1724 as 'an old, mean-built and very dirty city'. A century earlier, during the Civil War, one Roundhead sergeant said of the local people, 'The inhabitants are totally ignorant in the ways of God, and much addicted to drunkeness and other vice, but principally in swearing, so that the children that have scarcely learned to speak, do universally swear stoutly'.

▼ **Madley, The Church from the Vicarage c1955** M364008
Although once dedicated to St Dubricius, this church is now sanctified to the Nativity of the Virgin. A very large church for such a small community, building work started around 1120 and was not completed for 200 years.

◀ **Madley, The Altar, Church of the Nativity c1955** M364007
In 1942 Lieutenant-Commander Stephen Beattie, the son of the Rector of Madley, was awarded the Victoria Cross after his ship rammed the dock gates at St Nazaire. By the time the award was announced, however, Beattie was already in a POW camp in Germany. On receiving the news there, the German Camp Commandant held a special parade in his honour.

Madley
The Red Lion Inn c1955 M364001

Madley
The Red Lion c1965 M364010
It's only when you look closely at the detail that you realise that these
two photographs are indeed of the same place, so much has changed.
Funnily enough, those white lines for parking spaces painted in the
1960s have gone, although the area is still used for parking.

The South of the County

Longtown
The Greyhound Inn c1960 L536002
Longtown is exactly that – the settlement stretches along the road
for about a mile. The Greyhound Inn is now a private house. The
lean-to in the centre of the picture has been removed, so that the
timber work behind is totally uncovered.

Longtown, The School and Castle c1960 L536004
The school building in the centre of the photograph has been converted into private houses. Fortunately, however, for such a remote village, there is still a village school further up the road. Hidden amongst the trees are the remains of a real gem of a castle – its well worth a visit.

Longtown, The Castle c1960 L536008
Only the keep of the castle now survives. It was one of many castles built by the de Lacy family and was part of a network of castles throughout the area, used to control what was once wild, border country. In this photograph it is possible to see the small aperture that would once have been the garde robe, or toilet.

Longtown, Roman Road c1960 L536011
This is a very common sight in the hills of western Herefordshire, with the Border Collie dog herding a group of sheep. Border Collies are considered to be the most intelligent of dogs - it is always a thrill to watch them working.

Abbey Dore, Dore Abbey c1965 A1010
Like many abbeys and monasteries up and down the country, this former Cistercian monastery was dissolved in the reign of Henry VIII. Part of it was torn down immediately and what remained soon used as a glorified shelter for farm animals. It was restored by the 'Good Lord Scudamore' and re-consecrated in 1634. The restoration of the roof required the wood of 204 Herefordshire oak trees.

Ewyas Harold, Dulas Court c1965 E181021
This Victorian mansion sits in lovely grounds overlooking the Dulas (or 'black stream') Brook. At the time this photograph was taken Dulas Court was a home for retired musicians. However, having closed in 1994, it has recently become a residential care home for the elderly in general, not just musicians.

Ewyas Harold, The Village from the Castle Tump c1955 E181006
We tend to think that castles arrived in Britain with the Norman conquerors, but, in fact, they were already in existence. At Edward the Confessor's court, the influence of the Normans was so strong that the first so-called 'Norman' castles were actually built in the 1050s. One such (pre-Norman) 'Norman' castle originally stood on the site from which this photograph was taken.

▼ **Ewyas Harold, The Village c1955** E181005
In the days before almost everyone owned a car, quiet villages situated miles from the nearest town needed village shops able to supply all the essentials. The sign on the building on the far left advertised that Smith and Warren Stores were 'Grocers and Drapers, Corn and Seed Merchants and Wine and Ale Merchants'.

▼ **Ewyas Harold, Temple Bar Inn c1965** E181022
Ewyas Harold is a small village, miles from anywhere. However, in the 14th century it caused some disquiet. The Abbot at Gloucester complained that the monks sent to the village became so debased by the life there that, on their return home, they would inevitably corrupt the other monks. It does make one wonder just what was going on in this quiet, sleepy little village.

▲ **Ewyas Harold Dulas Road c1965**
E181014
Everything that wasn't sold at the Smith and Warren stores was probably sold by Michael Griffith instead. His sign advertises 'Medicines, Cosmetics, Baby Requirements, Paints and Wallpapers, Garden Sundries, Veterinary Remedies, Stationery and Toys'. The shop and the building beside it have since been converted into a private house.

◀ **Ewyas Harold
The Village c1960** E181012
The village is situated at
one end of the beautifully
named Golden Valley. It is
so called because the river
running through the valley
was known originally as the
Dwr, an old British word
simply meaning 'water'. To
the invading Normans, this
must have sounded like
their word 'd'or' meaning
'golden' - and their version
survived.

◀ **Much Dewchurch The Black Swan Annexe 1955** M183002
This building, as the sign suggests, was used to accommodate visitors to the Black Swan pub. The Black Swan, thought to date from the 14th century, is a lovely old hostelry in the heart of the village .

Much Dewchurch, Church of St David c1955 M183004

Much Dewchurch means 'the great or larger place with David's church', in contrast to Little Dewchurch a few miles to the east. Although named for St David, the David in question is not the same David who became the patron saint of Wales - although this is a common assumption in a village so close to the Welsh border.

Orcop Hill, The Fountain Inn c1955 O62008

There was once a Holy Thorn tree in Orcop that was said to have grown from a cutting from the staff of Joseph of Arimathea. Unfortunately, it was blown down in a gale in 1980. Of the five pubs that used to be found in the village, only the Fountain Inn, pictured here, survives today.

Peterstow The Post Office and Village Stores c1960 P173002

Although primarily a post office and village store, the signs tell us that teas were also served here 'neath the apple trees'. This serves as a reminder that once every household with enough space would have had an orchard somewhere in the garden.

▼ **Ross-on-Wye, Evening Reflections c1950** R57059
Described in 1972 by Maxwell Fraser in his book, 'Welsh Border Country' as 'one of those perfect English towns which are unsurpassable in their friendly atmosphere and old-world charm', Ross is beautifully situated overlooking the river. Notice all the boats in the foreground.

▼ **Ross-on-Wye, The Bridge c1965** R57127
What appears to be a statue projecting above the Wilton Bridge is, in fact, a sundial. The clock looks in four different directions and there are metal gnomons on each face. It is a most curious, but charming, feature.

▲ **Ross-on-Wye, The Hope and Anchor Hotel c1955** R57006
Overlooking a bridging point on the River Wye, Ross was an important meeting place from early days. The town has been described as doing most of its trade in the 17 inns that were once here. The large white building on the top of the hill is the Royal Hotel. It was built in 1837, just in time for the boom in tourism created by the new railways.

◀ **Ross-on-Wye**
The Wye from Thomas Blake Memorial Gardens c1960 R57110
Thomas Blake, who died in 1901, is known as 'Ross's Pious Benefactor' and actually did far more for the town than the better known John Kyrle. This view over the River Wye was taken before 1969 when the bypass and bridge were built. They now dominate this view.

**Ross-on-Wye
The Market in Broad
Street c1955** R57093
The style of the stalls
has changed somewhat
in the last 50 years and
there are now a
number of fast-food
vans in evidence.
Otherwise, the scene is
still very much the
same on market days,
with people trading
underneath the market
hall and spilling onto
the pavements around
about as they have
done here for
centuries.

**Ross-on-Wye
Market Square c1955**
R57063
Ross has been fortunate in its benefactors. The black and white building with the library sign was once the home of the 'Man of Ross', John Kyrle who died in 1714. He was given this nickname on account of his generosity to the town.

◀ **Ross-on-Wye**
Broad Street c1960
R57140
The library was donated by the town's other benefactor, Thomas Blake, in 1873 – it is located towards the bottom of Broad Street. He also had the Baptist church rebuilt in Broad Street.

Ross-on-Wye, Market Place c1955 R57062

The Market Hall, built of red sandstone, dates from the mid 1600s and stands on the site of an earlier hall. The carving between the windows is of a bust of Charles II. Today the upper floor is used as a Heritage Centre and houses a museum that tells the history of the town.

▼ Ross-on-Wye Gloucester Road c1960 R57112

This view looks along Gloucester Road from its junction with the High Street beside the Market Hall. The buildings on the far left of the picture, including the one marked National Provincial Bank, have been totally altered and are now unrecognisable from this photograph.

◄ Ross-on-Wye Gloucester Road c1955 R57142

Although difficult to read the name, the sign for the florist shop on the right reads 'Bridget Like Florist', and it is still 'Like's Florist' today. Notice the church beyond it - this is now an antiques centre and has the most glorious weather vane perched on the top of the roof.

Weston under Penyard, Weston Cross Inn c1965 W308031
This old stone pub dates from 1760. Today the building is almost totally covered with ivy. It is quite charming and, in my opinion, looks much more apt in a village that calls itself 'the garden village of south Herefordshire'.

Weston under Penyard, Post Office Corner c1955 W308003
The post office that gave this picture its name was based in the building on the left, which was also a village shop. Today there is no village shop, nor a post office. The building has been painted white and is now a private house.

Weston under Penyard, Gloucester Road c1955 W308001
The home of the 19th century author Mayne Reid was near here. Born in Ireland, he fought in the Mexican War (for which he received a pension from the American government) and used his experiences as the basis for the boys' adventure stories he wrote. He is also responsible for a treatise on the rules of croquet!

Goodrich, The River c1960 G31007
The Wye River is viewed here looking downstream from the Kerne Bridge. Within a short distance, the river becomes the border between Herefordshire and Gloucestershire. Further on, it subsequently becomes the border between England and Wales. The 11 mile walk between Ross-on-Wye to Monmouth has been described as 'the prettiest walk in England' (even if the last bit is in Wales).

▼ Goodrich, Kerne Bridge c1960 G31002

There was once a ferry crossing near here and it's said that the future King Henry IV was using the ferry when he received the news that his son had just been born at Monmouth. In grateful thanks for the safe delivery of his heir, Henry gave the boatman sole rights to the ferry and monies earned from it - a perk that the boatman's family were to enjoy for some centuries to come.

▼ Goodrich, Kerne Bridge c1960 G31005

The railway line was dismantled soon after this photograph was taken and you can no longer see the river as the bank is totally overgrown with trees. The buildings on the far bank stand on the site of Flanesford Priory, one of the many places of worship dissolved during the reign of Henry VIII.

▲ Whitchurch Cross Roads c1955

W582005

This junction is now a very busy dual carriageway. The building on the right – now demolished as part of the road widening scheme - advertises the Crown Hotel, on the other side of the road. The sign reads, 'The first hotel in England' - and we are, indeed, very close to the English/Welsh border.

◄ **Symonds Yat c1950**
S247019
This view across the River Wye portrays the deep valley the river has carved through the hills here. The river flows particularly swiftly at this point and is very popular with canoeists riding the rapids. The white building in the centre is the Saracen's Head pub.

Symonds Yat, The Old Ferry c1955 S247013
The ropes used for the ferry crossing are visible here. Once there were dozens of ferries crossing the Wye between Ross-on-Wye and Monmouth, now only two survive and they both operate along this stretch of the river, serving visitors to the region.

Symonds Yat, Wye Rapids Hotel c1965 S247115
Once one of two rival hotels facing each other across the valley, the Wye Rapids Hotel has since been demolished leaving the Royal Hotel as the main hotel in the valley.

Symonds Yat, Valdasso Café c1960 S247089
It is interesting to read the prices advertised beneath the Wall's ice cream 'Stop here and Buy Some' sign outside the café. A mineral drink, crush drink or milk shake was 6d (2p), and TT milk cost only 4d (2p). The pot of tea, however, is unpriced. 'TT milk', incidentally, was milk that had been Tuberculin tested.

Symonds Yat, The View c1965 S247139
This is described as the 'most famous viewpoint on the Wye'. Here the river can be seen actually flowing northwards before turning to the south once more. The river must travel for four miles in order to reach a point 500 yards away from where the photographer is standing.

Index

Abbey Dore 94

Bredenbury 61

Bredenbury Court 58-59, 60-61

Bromyard 61, 62-63, 64

Colwall 66, 67, 68

Dilwyn 46-47

Eardisland 20, 21, 22, 23

Eardisley 33, 34, 35

Eastnor 68, 69

Eastnor Castle 68-69

Ewyas Harold 95, 96-97

Goodrich 109, 110

Hereford 76-77, 78-79, 80-81, 82-83, 84-85, 86-87, 88-89

Hope under Dinmore 48, 49, 50-51

Kingsland 19, 20-21

Kington 29, 30-31, 32

Ledbury 70-71, 72-73, 74, 75

Leintwardine 16-17, 18-19

Leominster 52-53, 54-55, 56-57

Longtown 92, 93, 94

Lyonshall 28, 29

Madley 88, 89, 90, 91

Much Dewchurch 98-99

Orcop Hill 99

Pembridge 23, 24-25, 26-27, 28

Peterstow 99

Ross-on-Wye 100-101, 102-103, 104-105, 106-107

Sarnesfield 40

Symonds Yat 111, 112, 113, 114

Weobley 41, 42-43, 44, 45

Weston under Penyard 108, 109

Whitbourne 65

Whitchurch 110-111

Whitney 35, 36, 37

Winforton 38, 39, 40

www.francisfrith.co.uk

The Francis Frith Collection publishes over 100 new titles each year. A selection of those currently available is listed below. For latest catalogue please contact The Francis Frith Collection. **Town Books** 96 pages, approximately 75 photos. **County and Themed Books** 128 pages, approximately 135 photos (unless specified).

Accrington Old and New
Alderley Edge and Wilmslow
Amersham, Chesham and Rickmansworth
Andover
Around Abergavenny
Around Alton
Aylesbury
Barnstaple
Bedford
Bedfordshire
Berkshire Living Memories
Berkshire Pocket Album
Blackpool Pocket Album
Bognor Regis
Bournemouth
Bradford
Bridgend
Bridport
Brighton and Hove
Bristol
Buckinghamshire
Calne Living Memories
Camberley Pocket Album
Canterbury Cathedral
Cardiff Old and New
Chatham and the Medway Towns
Chelmsford
Chepstow Then and Now
Cheshire
Cheshire Living Memories
Chester
Chesterfield
Chigwell
Christchurch
Churches of East Cornwall
Clevedon
Clitheroe
Corby Living Memories
Cornish Coast
Cornwall Living Memories
Cotswold Living Memories
Cotswold Pocket Album
Coulsdon, Chipstead and Woodmanstern
County Durham
Cromer, Sheringham and Holt
Dartmoor Pocket Album
Derby
Derbyshire
Derbyshire Living Memories
Devon
Devon Churches
Dorchester

Dorset Coast Pocket Album
Dorset Living Memories
Dorset Villages
Down the Dart
Down the Severn
Down the Thames
Dunmow, Thaxted and Finchingfield
Durham
East Anglia Pocket Album
East Devon
East Grinstead
Edinburgh
Ely and The Fens
Essex Pocket Album
Essex Second Selection
Essex: The London Boroughs
Exeter
Exmoor
Falmouth
Farnborough, Fleet and Aldershot
Folkestone
Frome
Furness and Cartmel Peninsulas
Glamorgan
Glasgow
Glastonbury
Gloucester
Gloucestershire
Greater Manchester
Guildford
Hailsham
Hampshire
Harrogate
Hastings and Bexhill
Haywards Heath Living Memories
Heads of the Valleys
Heart of Lancashire Pocket Album
Helston
Herefordshire
Horsham
Humberside Pocket Album
Huntingdon, St Neots and St Ives
Hythe, Romney Marsh and Ashford
Ilfracombe
Ipswich Pocket Album
Isle of Wight
Isle of Wight Living Memories
King's Lynn
Kingston upon Thames
Lake District Pocket Album
Lancashire Living Memories
Lancashire Villages

Available from your local bookshop or from the publisher

The Francis Frith Collection Titles (continued)

Lancaster, Morecambe and Heysham Pocket Album
Leeds Pocket Album
Leicester
Leicestershire
Lincolnshire Living Memoires
Lincolnshire Pocket Album
Liverpool and Merseyside
London Pocket Album
Ludlow
Maidenhead
Maidstone
Malmesbury
Manchester Pocket Album
Marlborough
Matlock
Merseyside Living Memories
Nantwich and Crewe
New Forest
Newbury Living Memories
Newquay to St Ives
North Devon Living Memories
North London
North Wales
North Yorkshire
Northamptonshire
Northumberland
Northwich
Nottingham
Nottinghamshire Pocket Album
Oakham
Odiham Then and Now
Oxford Pocket Album
Oxfordshire
Padstow
Pembrokeshire
Penzance
Petersfield Then and Now
Plymouth
Poole and Sandbanks
Preston Pocket Album
Ramsgate Old and New
Reading Pocket Album
Redditch Living Memories
Redhill to Reigate
Richmond
Ringwood
Rochdale
Romford Pocket Album
Salisbury Pocket Album
Scotland
Scottish Castles
Sevenoaks and Tonbridge
Sheffield and South Yorkshire Pocket Album
Shropshire
Somerset
South Devon Coast
South Devon Living Memories
South East London
Southampton Pocket Album
Southend Pocket Album
Southport

Southwold to Aldeburgh
Stourbridge Living Memories
Stratford upon Avon
Stroud
Suffolk
Suffolk Pocket Album
Surrey Living Memories
Sussex
Sutton
Swanage and Purbeck
Swansea Pocket Album
Swindon Living Memories
Taunton
Teignmouth
Tenby and Saundersfoot
Tiverton
Torbay
Truro
Uppingham
Villages of Kent
Villages of Surrey
Villages of Sussex Pocket Album
Wakefield and the Five Towns Living Memories
Warrington
Warwick
Warwickshire Pocket Album
Wellingborough Living Memories
Wells
Welsh Castles
West Midlands Pocket Album
West Wiltshire Towns
West Yorkshire
Weston-super-Mare
Weymouth
Widnes and Runcorn
Wiltshire Churches
Wiltshire Living Memories
Wiltshire Pocket Album
Wimborne
Winchester Pocket Album
Windermere
Windsor
Wirral
Wokingham and Bracknell
Woodbridge
Worcester
Worcestershire
Worcestershire Living Memories
Wyre Forest
York Pocket Album
Yorkshire
Yorkshire Coastal Memories
Yorkshire Dales
Yorkshire Revisited

See Frith books on the internet at www.francisfrith.co.uk

FRITH PRODUCTS & SERVICES

Francis Frith would doubtless be pleased to know that the pioneering publishing venture he started in 1860 still continues today. Over a hundred and forty years later, The Francis Frith Collection continues in the same innovative tradition and is now one of the foremost publishers of vintage photographs in the world. Some of the current activities include:

Interior Decoration

Today Frith's photographs can be seen framed and as giant wall murals in thousands of pubs, restaurants, hotels, banks, retail stores and other public buildings throughout the country. In every case they enhance the unique local atmosphere of the places they depict and provide reminders of gentler days in an increasingly busy and frenetic world.

Product Promotions

Frith products are used by many major companies to promote the sales of their own products or to reinforce their own history and heritage. Frith promotions have been used by Hovis bread, Courage beers, Scots Porage Oats, Colman's mustard, Cadbury's foods, Mellow Birds coffee, Dunhill pipe tobacco, Guinness, and Bulmer's Cider.

Genealogy and Family History

As the interest in family history and roots grows world-wide, more and more people are turning to Frith's photographs of Great Britain for images of the towns, villages and streets where their ancestors lived; and, of course, photographs of the churches and chapels where their ancestors were christened, married and buried are an essential part of every genealogy tree and family album.

Frith Products

All Frith photographs are available Framed or just as Mounted Prints and Posters (size 23 x 16 inches). These may be ordered from the address below. From time to time other products - Address Books, Calendars, Table Mats, etc - are available.

The Internet

Already ninety thousand Frith photographs can be viewed and purchased on the internet through the Frith websites and a myriad of partner sites.

For more detailed information on Frith companies and products, look at these sites:

www.francisfrith.co.uk
www.francisfrith.com
(for North American visitors)

See the complete list of Frith Books at:

www.francisfrith.co.uk

This web site is regularly updated with the latest list of publications from The Francis Frith Collection. If you wish to buy books relating to another part of the country that your local bookshop does not stock, you may purchase on-line.

For further information, trade, or author enquiries please contact us at the address below:
The Francis Frith Collection, Frith's Barn, Teffont, Salisbury, Wiltshire, England SP3 5QP.
Tel: +44 (0)1722 716 376 Fax: +44 (0)1722 716 881 Email: sales@francisfrith.co.uk

See Frith books on the internet at www.francisfrith.co.uk

FREE PRINT OF YOUR CHOICE

Mounted Print
Overall size 14 x 11 inches (355 x 280mm)

Choose any Frith photograph in this book.
Simply complete the Voucher opposite and return it with your remittance for £2.25 (to cover postage and handling) and we will print the photograph of your choice in SEPIA (size 11 x 8 inches) and supply it in a cream mount with a burgundy rule line (overall size 14 x 11 inches).
Please note: **photographs with a reference number starting with a "Z" are not Frith photographs and cannot be supplied under this offer.**
Offer valid for delivery to one UK address only.

PLUS: Order additional Mounted Prints at HALF PRICE - £7.49 each (normally £14.99)
If you would like to order more Frith prints from this book, possibly as gifts for friends and family, you can buy them at half price (with no additional postage and handling costs).

PLUS: Have your Mounted Prints framed
For an extra £14.95 per print you can have your mounted print(s) framed in an elegant polished wood and gilt moulding, overall size 16 x 13 inches (no additional postage and handling required).

IMPORTANT!

These special prices are only available if you use this form to order. You must use the ORIGINAL VOUCHER on this page (no copies permitted). We can only despatch to one UK address. This offer cannot be combined with any other offer.

Send completed Voucher form to:
The Francis Frith Collection, Frith's Barn, Teffont, Salisbury, Wiltshire SP3 5QP

CHOOSE A PHOTOGRAPH FROM THIS BOOK

Voucher for FREE and Reduced Price Frith Prints

Please do not photocopy this voucher. Only the original is valid, so please fill it in, cut it out and return it to us with your order.

Picture ref no	Page no	Qty	Mounted @ £7.49	Framed + £14.95	Total Cost £
		1	Free of charge*	£	£
			£7.49	£	£
			£7.49	£	£
			£7.49	£	£
			£7.49	£	£
			£7.49	£	£
Please allow 28 days for delivery. Offer available to one UK address only			* Post & handling		£2.25
			Total Order Cost		£

Title of this book . . . .

I enclose a cheque/postal order for £ . . . .
made payable to 'The Francis Frith Collection'

OR please debit my Mastercard / Visa / Maestro card details below

Card Number

Issue No (Maestro only)   Valid from (Maestro)

Expires   Signature

Name Mr/Mrs/Ms . . . .
Address . . . .
. . . .
. . . .
. . . . Postcode . . . .
Daytime Tel No . . . .
Email . . . .

ISBN: 1-84589-107-4   Valid to 31/12/08

Can you help us with information about any of the Frith photographs in this book?

We are gradually compiling an historical record for each of the photographs in the Frith archive. It is always fascinating to find out the names of the people shown in the pictures, as well as insights into the shops, buildings and other features depicted.

If you recognize anyone in the photographs in this book, or if you have information not already included in the author's caption, do let us know. We would love to hear from you, and will try to publish it in future books or articles.

Our production team

Frith books are produced by a small dedicated team at offices in the converted Grade II listed 18th-century barn at Teffont near Salisbury, illustrated above. Most have worked with the Frith Collection for many years. All have in common one quality: they have a passion for the Frith Collection. The team is constantly expanding, but currently includes:

Paul Baron, Jason Buck, John Buck, Ruth Butler, Heather Crisp, David Davies, Louis du Mont, Isobel Hall, Lucy Hart, Julian Hight, Peter Horne, James Kinnear, Karen Kinnear, Tina Leary, Stuart Login, Sue Molloy, Glenda Morgan, Wayne Morgan, Sarah Roberts, Kate Rotondetto, Dean Scource, Eliza Sackett, Terence Sackett, Sandra Sampson, Adrian Sanders, Sandra Sanger, Julia Skinner, David Turner, Miles Murray, Lewis Taylor, Shelley Tolcher, Lorraine Tuck, Miranda Tunnicliffe, Amanita Wainwright and Ricky Williams.